CAT PLACES

Pomegranate
SAN FRANCISCO

Pomegranate Communications, Inc.
Box 6099
Rohnert Park, CA 94927
www.pomegranate.com

Pomegranate Europe, Ltd.
Fullbridge House, Fullbridge
Maldon, Essex CM9 4LE
England

© 1992 Alfred Gescheidt

ISBN 1-56640-025-2
Pomegranate Catalog No. A622

Pomegranate publishes books of postcards on a wide range of subjects.
Please write to the publisher for more information.

Cover design by Shannon Lemme

Printed in Korea

07 06 05 04 03 02 01 00   17 16 15 14 13 12 11 10 9

To facilitate detachment of the postcards from this book, fold each card along its perforation line before tearing.

The places cats prefer
Are those where they can purr
On a window ledge
Or a garden hedge
Anywhere they can be demure.

There is no place *not* theirs
Be it on the table or under the stairs
But they will not abide
No place to hide
From other cats putting on airs.

A cat will be circumspect
In deciding which place to select
But once settled there
It will no longer care
And will nap—instead of reflect.

—Anonymous, c. 1915

cat places

Photograph by Alfred Gescheidt

POMEGRANATE　BOX 6099　ROHNERT PARK, CA 94927

cat places

Photograph by Alfred Gescheidt

POMEGRANATE BOX 6099 ROHNERT PARK CA 94927

cat places

Photograph by Alfred Gescheidt

POMEGRANATE BOX 6099 ROHNERT PARK CA 94927

cat places

Photograph by Alfred Gescheidt

POMEGRANATE BOX 6099 ROHNERT PARK CA 94927

cat places

Photograph by Alfred Gescheidt

POMEGRANATE   BOX 6099   ROHNERT PARK CA 94927

cat places

Photograph by Alfred Gescheidt

POMEGRANATE   BOX 6099   ROHNERT PARK CA 94927

cat places

Photograph by Alfred Gescheidt

POMEGRANATE   BOX 6099   ROHNERT PARK CA 94927

cat places

Photograph by Alfred Gescheidt

POMEGRANATE BOX 6099 ROHNERT PARK CA 94927

cat places

Photograph by Alfred Gescheidt

POMEGRANATE BOX 6099 ROHNERT PARK CA 94927

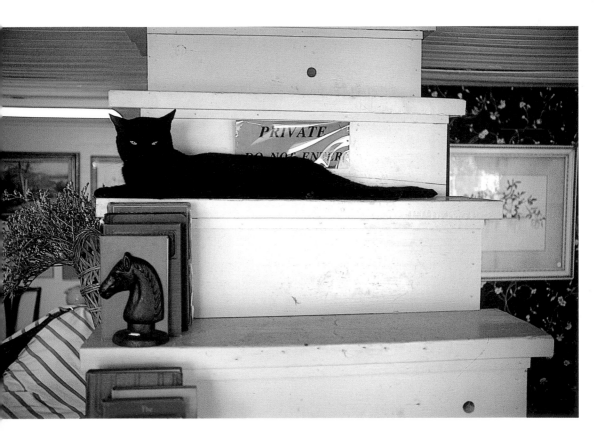

cat places

Photograph by Alfred Gescheidt

POMEGRANATE BOX 6099 ROHNERT PARK CA 94927

cat places

Photograph by Alfred Gescheidt

POMEGRANATE   BOX 6099   ROHNERT PARK, CA 94927

cat places

Photograph by Alfred Gescheidt

POMEGRANATE BOX 6099 ROHNERT PARK CA 94927

cat places

Photograph by Alfred Gescheidt

POMEGRANATE BOX 6099 ROHNERT PARK CA 94927

cat places

Photograph by Alfred Gescheidt

POMEGRANATE BOX 6099 ROHNERT PARK CA 94927

cat places

Photograph by Alfred Gescheidt

POMEGRANATE BOX 6099 ROHNERT PARK CA 94927

cat places

Photograph by Alfred Gescheidt

POMEGRANATE   BOX 6099   ROHNERT PARK CA 94927

cat places

Photograph by Alfred Gescheidt

POMEGRANATE BOX 6099 ROHNERT PARK CA 94927

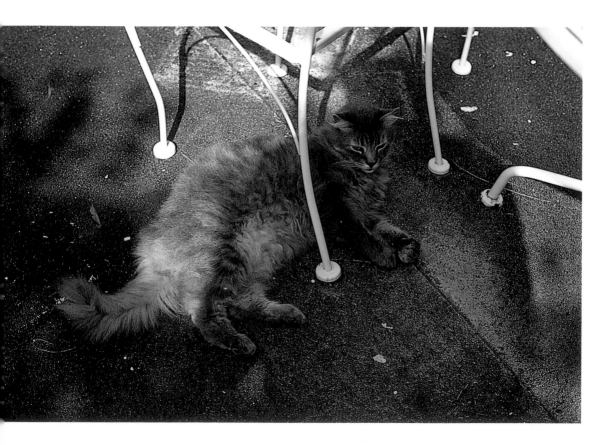

cat places

Photograph by Alfred Gescheidt

POMEGRANATE   BOX 6099   ROHNERT PARK, CA 94927